M.I.N.D. YOUR BUSINESS

DONISHIA C. YARDE

Copyright © 2018 by OKEY Consulting Group, LLC: First Edition, 2018
OKEY Consulting Group, LLC
223 East Lake Ave
Auburndale, FL 33823

Library of Congress Cataloging-in-Publication Data

Donishia C. Yarde
M.I.N.D. Your Business
Edited by: Jenna Sims
Published by: OKEY Consulting Group, LLC

10 9 8 7 6 5 4 3 2 1

Printed in the United States of America

Note: This book is intended only as a real-life testimony of the life and times of Donishia Yarde. Readers are advised to consult a professional before making any life changes. The reader assumes all responsibility for the consequences of any actions taken based on the information presented in this book. The information in this book is based on the author's research and experience. Every attempt has been made to ensure that the information is accurate; however, the author cannot accept liability for any errors that may exist. The facts and theories about life are subject to interpretation, and the conclusions and recommendations presented here may not agree with other interpretations.

TABLE OF CONTENTS

INTRODUCTION

You think your life was hard? Let me tell you, mine was too. I've battled with so many things over the years, and the battle continues. In times when we face some type of spiritual warfare, we must always remind ourselves that victory is near. Life is no piece of cake. It never will be. As long as you are breathing, you will be tested in every area. You can't allow life's test to beat you down. You have to be willing to fight the good fight and build your life regardless of adversities thrown in your way.

I come from nothing. I've lived in some rough areas and tough situations. I've lived with rats and roaches. I've seen it all and have been through it all. Anyone who knows me personally can vouch for me on that. But, God made a way. Through it all, I came out on top and I want to share that journey with you. There is much to learn in the transformation from nothing to something. From being evicted time and time again as a child in my parent's home, to building businesses that are successful in every right, there were many difficult and enlightening lessons along the way. I want to reveal the inside story - the "behind the scenes." I want to hand you the knowledge that no one gave me. I learned the hard way. I had to make a conscious decision to prevail. I now employ fifteen people, and I'm sure along the way, some of those very people thought I was crazy. But there's a method to the madness. I want to share my methods with you. There's still so much I wish to do and I'm still working on the resources to do it, but it will be done. I'll share those lessons with you in my next book. Buckle up. I'm taking you behind the scenes of a businesswoman!

CHAPTER 1

Your Past Prepared You!

Most people run and hide from their past. Some even pack the past away in a place where they do not have to confront it. I admit, I run from mine at times too. It can be painful and uncomfortable to look back over your life in retrospect. You've seen some things, done some things, and gone through some things that are unspeakable. We're human. We all struggle, but in different ways. We each would have a story to tell if we sat down to tell it. I don't think a stranger would even believe my whole story if I told it all. I look at myself today and what I've endured, and I can't believe I'm still here and functioning on the level I am. It gets that deep for me. One day I'll tell my full story, but I don't think the world is ready just yet. I have much more to do and then I'll fill you in on the full details. Go on this journey with me, and when we get to that book, you'll be glad you read every book before it.

Look at your past. Look at the pain. Look at your mistakes. Now pull the lessons from your experiences. What did they teach you? What did they turn you into? How did they shape you and make you who you are today? Have you used the pain or has it used you? Have you thought about it, prayed about it or talked about it? Do you ever remind yourself of the things you've suffered and the things you've overcome? Do you take inventory over your life to see if the past is still winning in the present? Are you allowing your past to make you live a lie? Or are you living a secret? I can't judge you for any way you've dealt with your pain. I'm still dealing with mine. We are all still dealing with our pain; it is not an overnight process. I ran and ran; I may still be running. It's a journey, it's a process and the truth is hard to tell. The truth is hard to confront. You have to confront it day by day. It has to come out at some point, even if it's only in the mirror. You can't let it break you. Let it make you. Let it push you into greatness and bring something out of you that will set you and others free. Pain can become purpose. You can take the bad things and turn them into good things. It all depends on how you handle it. I've lost loved ones over and over again. Things were done to me that no one believes but God. I've cried countless nights. I've been down and out. I was suicidal as a child for quite a while. I went through so much growing up that my childhood is a whole book in itself. Maybe you've gone through some things in private that even family and friends can't believe. Maybe you've done some things that you plan to take to your grave. You have to use everything in your life to make yourself better. You can't let anything lie idle. You can't let anything work against you; it has to work for you. You have to coach yourself. In addition to the life coaching, counseling and therapy, you still have to fix you. You can't leave all the work up to someone else. You have to look yourself in the mirror and vow to get stronger. Commit yourself to growth.

Tell yourself this:

I didn't go through all of this for nothing. Everything I've gone through was intended to make me stronger and wiser. My mistakes were for a reason. Every bad thing that has happened to me, I'm going to turn into a positive. I refuse to live as a victim to my past. I refuse to lie down and let life beat me up. I forgive everyone who hurt me. I now know they hurt me because they were hurting. I forgive myself for blaming myself, for hating myself, and for trying to hurt myself. I will succeed in life. I will be victorious. There are no more excuses. I have to get better. I have to keep going. I have to keep growing. I won't lose in life; I will win. People may doubt me, but I believe in myself. People may talk about it, but I can't hear the naysayers. Life is meant to be lived, and I vow to live it to the fullest. I can't give up on myself or my dreams.

You have to set yourself free. You have to claim the victory in your life. As a child, I suffered a lot. I suffered in my neighborhood and in school. I was a troubled child. I would scream, yell, fight and cry. I internalized so much. I became withdrawn at some point. I started to let my imagination run wild. I started to dream big dreams. Dreaming became my escape from the pain of life. I wasn't the pretty girl. I felt ugly and I was called ugly. I was darker than many others. I was long and skinny when other girls were blossoming. I was a rough and tough tomboy when other girls were becoming more feminine. I couldn't get into the girly things even though I tried. I was a fighter. I felt every bit of pain and I tried to deliver some pain. The world was beating me up, and after lying down to be ran over didn't kill me, I got up and started to fight back. The world doesn't want to see you win. You have to want to see you win. You have to get the lessons and then turn them into blessings.

What does the pain teach you? It teaches you that you're a survivor. If what you've gone through didn't kill you, its purpose was to make you stronger. I shouldn't be where I am today. I could be in prison, or worse yet, I could be in the grave. My surroundings and my life could have made me a statistic, but God had other plans. If you are reading this, God has plans for you. This didn't happen by accident. This book didn't land in your hands on accident. This is divine intervention to call you out of the place of complacency and push you into greatness. It's time for your next level. It's time for you to go higher. It's time for you to get better than ever before. You're about to be a new release that no one has ever seen before. They will be floored. They won't have words to describe the growth in you. Maybe you're successful in your own right, but you've gotten complacent. It's time for more! You're the mayor? It's time to be the senator! You're the city manager? It's time to run the county! You can accomplish more and become more no matter how much you have or haven't already done. You have to be willing to go the extra mile where there is no traffic. You have to be willing to come out of your shell and see the world with new eyes. You can't lie dormant anymore; you have to rise up. You've been in training for the next level all your life. It's that time.

What do mistakes teach you? They teach you that you are human. You've made mistakes. Some things you owned up to, and others, you want to take to your grave. You have to look at your mistakes and vow to be a better person. Ask for forgiveness from those you've hurt, harmed or wronged. Don't live a lie; walk in your truth. Ask them to forgive you and tell them how you've changed. Have you changed? Are you still changing? What have you done to change? How much coaching, counseling, or therapy have you sought and completed? Even if that came from the Holy

Bible, how often do you read it? Don't let your mistakes haunt you. Forgive yourself and heal. Vow to be a new and different person. Don't give anyone anything negative to say about you. Let them eat their words if they're talking bad about you today. Don't be a victim to your mistakes. Trust that you can rebuild and grow into a new person. Those mistakes are there to teach you that you're human and you have flaws. They serve their purpose to keep you humble and forever on a journey of growth and change. You're not a monster. You're not an idiot. You're not worthless. You're not useless. You're not the worst society has to offer. You can't believe the lies you sometimes tell yourself. You have to seek the truth.

No matter how dark your past, there is a bright future for you. I've seen abuse victims like myself turn it around. I've seen drug dealers turn it around. I've seen low self-esteem rise to high self-esteem. I've seen drastic changes for the better over and over. No one can tell me that people can't change. I see change happen every day. We have the ability to change our lives and to live our best lives. You have to know that and believe that.

You've experienced pain. You've made mistakes. Things

have happened to you and you've brought some other things on yourself. That's all a part of life and you have to embrace that fact. Your past has prepared you for your future. It's time to make it happen.

Today, I'm running a purpose-based business. I own several group homes, a fingerprinting business, a real-estate investment company, and a consulting company. My past prepared me for this moment in my life and I see it as just the beginning. I've had millions in assets and millions in debt. I've seen both sides of it. I've made many mistakes and I've learned from them. I allowed my pain to give me a heart for people. My pain led to my purpose because it made me feel lowly and empty. I learned at the bottom how people feel at the lowest point in their lives. It made me look at the world differently. It gave me a passion to serve those in need. I don't prey on the weak. I pray for the weak. There's a big difference and my pain put me in the place to understand that.

The mistakes I made showed me that I'm daring and I'm a risk taker. I live and think outside of the box and I go after what I want. I'm not afraid to fail. I'm not afraid to lose. If you let someone else describe me, they might say I'm a little crazy, I dream too big, they say. I'm all over the place, they say. I need to slow down, they say. I need to focus on one thing at a time, they say. They say this and they say that. They say it all because they're not me. They don't have the pain and purpose I have so they don't understand me and how I make moves. They never will get it. I don't care if they get it now because I know they'll see it later.

CHAPTER 2

It's A Journey

Nothing profound happens overnight. As badly as we want it to, it will take some time. The gift is innate in you. You possess what it takes to reach your highest potential. You can realize your dreams if you keep working for them. You may climb to the mountaintop and circle back before finding your niche. You may feel lost at times, but you must keep putting one foot in front of the other. Trust your process and don't lose hope.

Recognize your gifts early on the journey. Count your wins. I remember I was working at a call center. I did my job to the best of my ability. My personality is to lead in any situation. I naturally think outside of the box and voice my opinions. Before I knew it, I was earning $1,000 a week in commission. I saw a supervisor position become available and I applied for it. I was 16 or 17 years old earning supervisor wages and leading the call room floor. I recognized my gifting early. I felt called to lead. I knew I wanted to be a boss, but I didn't know how I would make it happen.

I went through three or four jobs before I really got settled into something purposeful and worthwhile. It takes time. It takes patience. You have to be willing to go through some things to get where you want to be. I worked in the trucking business too. I was a dispatcher and running my own trucks for years. I saw an opportunity and I seized it. No matter what position I was in, I always found a way to win. I had to learn the system and then master it. I'm a risk taker. I push the envelope. I don't let anyone box me in or limit what I can do. Everything you do in life will be preparation for the big job. You can't take any job for granted. Everything is an opportunity to learn and grow. You may not find your way overnight, but with perseverance, you'll eventually hit your stride.

Who are you learning from? Who are you willing to listen

to? Who is your mentor? Surround yourself with people who are successful and listen to their conversations. Learn how they talk, how they think, and how they operate in business. It's important to identify people who can help you grow. You have to be open-minded to meet new people. I was learning from my bosses and coworkers. I always paid attention to the people working around me. Every relationship, every interaction, and every partnership can teach you something, even if it's what not to do. You have to be open-minded and look for the lessons. If you feel like you already know it all, you'll fail time and time again.

There were times I got fed up while working with other people. I've had bosses I felt I couldn't learn from, but I still was looking for lessons. I've had coworkers who looked down on me and laughed at me behind my back. They heard my dreams of owning my own companies and making lots of money and they thought I was crazy. I remember days of not wanting to get up and go to someone else's job. I wanted my own but I wasn't sure what I'd do. I had to stay the course. I would talk to people in my circle sometimes and they would tell me I was dreaming too big. They told me I was moving too fast and needed to slow down. I felt like a fish out of water. I knew deep down I wanted more, but I didn't know how to get it. It was not about being filthy rich. For me, it was about owning my own business and working for myself. I knew the money would come, but I wanted peace of mind and happiness.

There will be times when you start to feel like a pawn on a chessboard. You'll be beat up and feel lost or out of place. You have to take a deep breath and start coaching yourself to be the best version of yourself. You have to remind yourself of your dreams, goals and your greatness. You can't get weary. Run the race. Stay the course. It's coming when you least expect it. No matter how I felt on the inside, I never let people see me sweat. I made a point to check my attitude and make sure I was carrying myself in the best light possible. People wanted to teach me. I had help coming from many different directions. I was focused. I always sounded like I knew more than I did, but it was my ambition and drive speaking.

You can't allow yourself to get down for long. You'll feel down on certain days but you have to keep the vision clear. Take some time to write down your goals. Get a poster board and add pictures that represent your dream job and your goals. Look at that vision board every day and visualize it in your mind before you leave home. Unlock your mind and dream bigger. You have to want more for yourself. You may have to go through five jobs to get there. I know people who have had over 25 jobs in their adult life and are just now stepping into their purpose and calling. It takes considerable time. There is no blueprint for us when we are born, unless our parents have already done it and paved the way. In most cases, we have to find our way as we go. Don't feel like you have to have it all figured out on day one.

Pay close attention to your surroundings and your interactions. Your dreams and plans could be staring you in the face. You could be talking to the person who will teach you everything you need to know about the next level. Your smile could attract an investor. Your conversation could win you a mentor. Always be mindful and always be present. Blessings come in many different forms and at many different times. Don't kill your dreams with self-doubt and self-pity.

If I had become complacent, I wouldn't be writing this book right now. I would have stayed at the call center where the money seemed great. I was a kid earning $48,000 a year. There aren't many people who can say that. I didn't show all of my money. I like to buy nice things, but I didn't do much flaunting. I knew I would climb even higher. I knew I wanted more out of life. I could have stayed in the trucking business. Complacency is your enemy. Keep serving in every way you can. You may be serving someone else's dream and then discover your own in that process.

As they say, a thousand-mile journey begins with one step. You have to be willing to go on this journey. If you don't enjoy your current level, keep dreaming about where you want to be. Don't just dream - make a plan. Start developing your plan so you can hit the ground running and gain steam for your dream.

I never enjoyed working for someone else. It was my goal to surpass my boss. I wanted to be my boss's boss. I didn't know how it would happen but I knew it would. I had to read, study, and absorb as much information as I could. I was learning myself through my mistakes. Because I wasn't afraid to live, I had made enough mistakes to learn what made me tick. I saw myself in so many different situations, and each situation taught me something different about myself. That was the joy of living a full life.

If you find yourself on a job you don't want, you can do something about it. Go to work with a song on your heart. Right before work, listen to your favorite song and sing it all day long. Make yourself smile at everyone. Show kindness to others. Don't be a snob and give people a reason to hate you. Some will hate you anyway, but at least you can say it wasn't because of you. Smile in their faces. Work like it's the best job in the world. Make them want to promote you and put the power in your hands. If you bust your butt, they'll want to move you up the ladder. If your dream isn't ready to get off the ground, take the promotion and learn even more. Balance your job with your dream. Learn how to work for them and work for yourself at the same time. You may have to dedicate your days off to your dream. Don't complain on your job. Change the way you look at it and find the good in every situation.

Your goal should be to leave a legacy everywhere you go. Your coworkers may one day become your employees. You don't want to be hated. Your current boss may become your future employee. Make your name great. You will make mistakes. You will burn some bridges. You have to cut your losses and get better. Your good can outweigh the bad. Don't get caught up in the backbiting and gossiping. Make sure you can fly above the haters, spectators and perpetrators. You're going places. You're planning big things. Don't get caught up with the bottom feeders along the way.

Take your journey and keep going. No matter how bad or how good you feel you're doing, it's all a part of the journey. Don't miss any experiences and don't miss any lessons. Keep believing and keep pressing toward your ultimate goal.

CHAPTER 3

Fill The Void In The Marketplace

F ind the need and meet it. There is something in you that can change the world. You don't have to change the entire world, but you can change the world around you. You can get in position to have a positive effect in your community. The things you've endured and experienced have prepared you to serve somewhere and be of relevance in a way that will leave a lasting impact. You have to find that space and fill it with your gifts and influence. You have to create a lane if one doesn't exist. You can't trust that opportunities will fall into your lap. It's up to you to get in the marketplace and fill the void.

Today, I run several group homes. I saw a need in this space. I helped a lady get her company off the ground. I wrote the policies and conducted all the research. I learned then that I'm a helper. I'm a catalyst to others. I was operating like a consultant at that point, but that wasn't my title. That is exactly why I've started OKEY Consulting Group! I'm finding the needs and meeting them. At that time, I didn't really know what I wanted to do. I just wanted to be effective and to have purpose and meaning in my life. That job provided that for me. Once I got in there behind the scenes, I saw room for improvement. I wasn't the boss though. I could only do so much because of the limitations of my position. I've always believed in leading from wherever you are, but if it's not your ship, you can't be the captain. I had all the influence that I could have, but it wasn't enough.

One day I decided it was time for me to step out on my own and do my own things. I branched off and started working on my own group home. I saw the space needed someone who genuinely cared. They needed someone who could make a real difference in the lives of the clientele. It had to be me to do it. I've always felt like, if it's meant to be, it's up to me. I rolled up my sleeves and I got to work. It wasn't easy. I faced rejection after rejection. I couldn't really find much help. I had to bust my butt. I remember an agency telling me they didn't have a need for anymore group homes. They didn't believe in me right away. They thought I was too young, maybe too much of other things too. I remained prayerful and diligent in my efforts. I begged them for one chance, just a chance to prove I had a vision and could be the best in the field.

After some persistence and prayer, I got my breakthrough. They let me in. They got me set up and I hit the ground running. I won't lie; it was not easy. Anything worth having is worth working for. I realized that I was needed in this space. I had to set up shop and be an example for others to follow. I want to run my company with excellence. I want to provide excellent service. I want to be the best at everything I do. I don't want to settle for mediocrity. Being a minority woman, those are two battles I have to fight at times. Many people don't want to talk about it or admit it, but there is prejudice in the world. It's not everyone, but sometimes the person you need to sign off on your paper may be the person who doesn't feel like you deserve the position you're aspiring to fulfill. In addition to that, I'm still considered young in business. Being in my early 30's can make some people look at me with doubt. It's almost as if they see me as a child, incapable of doing what I've set out to do. It can be daunting at times. Things won't always go your way when you're trying to fill a void.

I kept hitting roadblocks. I had to hear "NO" often. I was dreaming too big and too fast. But I knew I had to stay the course. My main focus is integrity. That's why my company is called Integrity Care Homes. I noticed early on that the industry lacked the level of integrity I felt I could bring. So I committed myself to it. My goal is to set my company apart from all others. I don't want to be lumped in and judged with the industry as a whole. For some people, their goals and aspirations are centered on a paycheck. I don't focus on the money; I focus on the care. The monetary rewards are only good to me if I'm operating with integrity. They money isn't the focus; it's the byproduct of my focus. By doing quality work, I get to help more consumers. That mindset built my company's reputation and we became known as one of the top providers in the area. If I would have entered the industry with the same mindset as some others, I wouldn't have been able to build what we've built. One group home became two. Then two became three. Then three became four and so on. I could have called my company Extra Mile, because that's another one of my personal beliefs - going the extra mile. I saw so many people doing just enough to get by. The bare minimum doesn't cut it for me. I want to be exemplary. I want to be extraordinary. I don't want to be average and just fit in. I have to stand out and do more. I have to go further and be better than the rest.

When you see a need in the marketplace you know you can fill, be that person. Don't worry about the naysayers. Don't worry about those who won't help you. Don't think about the obstacles. Be determined to complete your goals. Don't settle where you are if you know you can be more and have more. The world needs your gifts and you have to be willing to share them. If you don't do it, someone else will. They can never be you. Whatever you want out of life, you can get it by using your gifts. Don't trap yourself or box yourself in. Be willing to go further and to do more.

I decided not to stop, but to keep going. It started with the group homes, but now I run three companies and I have a couple more in the works. I believe we have to aspire to inspire until we expire. I don't believe we should take any gifts to the grave. The most gifted place in the world is the graveyard. I refuse to be another statistic. Outside of my three companies, I decided to birth this book. It may not be the best book you read in your lifetime, but if one sentence inspires you, my goal was accomplished. Who is to say I can't be a business owner, author and speaker? To the average mind, it may be doing "too much," but when you start thinking differently, you realize that you can do it all. You can tap into your dreams and provide something the world has been missing. It doesn't mean that you have to start something that has never been done before, because that's highly unlikely. But you just have to do it the to the best of your ability and be at your best. It's your life and you can live it how you wish to live it. Who is to say what you can't do and who you can't be? Truthfully, only you hold that power.

Be willing to be different. Be willing to be bold. Be willing to stand out and allow people to say whatever they want about you. As long as you know you're living your truth, you are doing your job. Some will hate you. Some will love you. That comes with the territory. You can't worry about spectators. They are paying you to watch you work. They'll be there, so keep going. You have to know there will be failures. You'll blow up your bubble and it may burst. Oh well, blow up another one. Even in the midst of my success, I have failures. I've made countless mistakes. I've won along the way and I've lost along the way. I've mishandled my personal finances by spending or giving away too much. I've lost a few friends and family over money or business issues. I've had to let employees go, and there have been days I'm sure my employees hated me. Nothing was ever intentional but it's a part of life. You will fail. You will make mistakes. You just have to be committed to learning from every experience.

There is something about you that makes you special. There could be lots of things that make you special. Your special make up is needed somewhere in this world. Find that place. Most likely, you're already being drawn to it, but you're ignoring it subconsciously. Pay closer attention. Look at the things that are pulling you. How are you spending your time? What are you doing the most? That area of your life is a gift or a passion and there's something to it. There's more you can do with it. Find that and pursue it relentlessly. You can't give up on your dreams. You can't count yourself out and feel that it's not for you. Believe that the space has been reserved for you, because in all honesty, it has. It's yours and no one can take your place and do exactly what you can do in that space. Don't be afraid to try and fail. Get back up and try again. When you hear "no," ask again.

I'm asking you not to cheat us of your gift. I'm doing all I can and I will continue to do more. I hope my efforts will inspire others to do more too. We all have a task to complete before we move on to the next level; don't ignore your calling. Don't let the world tell you no if your heart is telling you yes. It's for you. It can be yours. Just be bold enough to take the first step to make it happen.

CHAPTER 4

Pick Your Team Wisely

Your team is essential. In the beginning, it may be only you. Keep it that way until you absolutely have to bring others along. Picking the right people to be on your team can get very tricky. There are certain qualities you have to look for in team members. There are also certain qualities you must possess to attract the right people to your team. Your team doesn't have to be paid staff right out the gate. They may be like-minded people who have the same type of vision. As a team, you can dream and plan together. You can push one another. Don't rush it. Take your time while building a team because the people you put around you can make you or break you.

When looking for team members, I look for certain qualities and characteristics. I want humble people on my team. Humility takes you a long way. To be humble means that you acknowledge you don't know it all, but you're willing to learn. It also means you treat others the way you want to be treated. Humble people don't walk around with their noses in the clouds and looking down on others. These are the people you can trust on your team because you know they care about others as much or even more than they care about themselves. Humility is a necessity for me and it's one of the first traits I look for in another person. Some people can fake humility, but I've been there before, so I know what it looks like. I can read right through an arrogant person who is trying to pretend to be humble. Humility doesn't mean the person isn't confident. Confidence and humility go hand in hand. Arrogance actually comes from weakness and insecurity trying to pose as something else. I'm aware of the difference between arrogance and confidence. Humble people can be genuinely confident. I'm always paying attention to the attitudes on my team, and I can't tolerate anything less than the best. It's very important to me to have the right type of people on my team because they become an extension of me. If I can't trust them, I can't count on them. If I can't count on them, I should just close the doors of my business because we are doomed to fail.

Another quality I look for in team members is ambition. I want my team to be driven. If you have dreams, goals, and aspirations of your own, I know you'll be a motivated worker for mine. Those people with ambition can sometimes get sidetracked, but if I can get them to see the vision, they really become the ideal team member. Ambition doesn't have to be outside of the workplace. A person can be ambitious about the work. They may want to be the best and to climb the ranks. They may even want to be in my shoes one day. I'm okay with that. That lets me know I can expect diligence and for them to work their butts off to learn all they can. Ambition is important to me because it's a driving force. Complacent people won't get much done and they'll always look for ways to cut corners. In my business, I can't tolerate people who want to take shortcuts. In my line of work, we can't cut any corners because we have lives at stake. We have to be very focused and driven so we can accomplish our goals in the workplace. If a person starts slacking, things can go terribly wrong and my business is on the line.

Another thing I'm looking for in team members is team spirit. I want to know that this person can get along with other people and bring good energy to the house and the office. My team is working in the house with clients in need, and if their energy isn't right, it will ruin the home. I need people who are upbeat in a genuine way and really want to work together to make things happen. I can't have know-it-alls, showstoppers, and one-man shows. It just won't work. We have to communicate, coordinate, and execute the game plan. I need to know that the person I'm communicating with can hang up the phone and execute the plan of our agreement. If they hang up and do their own thing, there can be a major price for me to pay.

Another quality I look for in team members is natural intelligence. I want to make sure my team has common sense. It's great to be book smart, but I need someone who can think outside the box and be effective in tough situations. If a person relies too much on their degrees and formal training, they won't do well in the group home environment. We have to be able to adapt to different situations and use common sense and critical thinking skills to solve problems. We can't throw a book or label at everything. It takes some real work to make things run smoothly. We have to be able to relate to multiple personality types, so it takes a person with a diverse background of experiences to be able to do that. If I notice a person is judgmental, prejudiced, jaded, or out of touch with the real world, I can't throw them in the mix. It takes tact, class, and ingenuity to get the job done. I have a formal education, but I was self-taught well before that and can adapt to any situation with any type of person. I have a lot of experiences in my life to pull from and I don't expect everyone to have lived through all that I did, but I'm looking for something close.

You can't pick a team based on superficial things. A lot of business owners pick team members based on education, looks or association. You can't choose suitable people by reading certificates or looking only at their physical appearance. You have to be open-minded and realize that your key team members may come in many different forms. Some will be formally educated, and some will only have high school diplomas. Some will be tall.

Some will be short. Some will come from poverty. Some will come from wealth. There will be a mix and you have to be open minded to that. Don't box a person into a specific category based on their race, gender or past. Allow them to show you who they are, and then judge them based on that interaction.

Of course in my line of work with group homes, I have to have a team for it to work. In your line of work, you may be able to work alone for the most part and have independent contractors help you out. Don't feel like you have to have a big office and salaried employees to be considered successful. Be okay starting where you are with what you have. A team will come together, and it may look different from a team in a different industry.

I've made hiring mistakes before. I've hired thieves. I've hired people who didn't care about the company. I've hired liars. I've hired people who wanted to be in my shoes and let their jealousy affect their performance. These mistakes in the hiring department have strengthened my discernment. Because of those mistakes, I now know what to look for in quality team members. I'm also not afraid to let someone go if they get complacent or out of line. You have to realize that not everything is permanent.

People may change over time. You have to be okay with letting people go if that's what is needed for the greater good. Don't get stuck holding onto people who need to be let go. It's okay to make mistakes, realize the mistake, and then make changes. It happens and we call it "life."

Be careful of your choices for a team. Make sure to keep it purely business, even if you bring family or friends into the fold. I work with my sister, stepfather, significant other, and friends. I like it, but sometimes I have to put people in check and remind them that it's my business and we have to *keep* it business. Hopefully, family and friends will understand and respect you. Once you show them you don't play any games, they'll get the picture, and if not, they have to be let go. Nothing can come before your business if you want it to succeed. You can't let anyone run your business into the ground in the name of family or friendship. You have to be able to put your foot down and put standards in place. One of the biggest problems I see with CEO's is they allow their friends and family to undermine their business. You can't be afraid to let people go. Otherwise, the industry will let you go.

CHAPTER 5

Empower Your Friends And Family

Y ou can't be the only one who makes it. Others may not become as successful as you, but you want them to experience a certain level of success. You have to identify which friends and family members want more out of life and then connect with them. In the beginning, you might inspire one another, but if you start to pull away in your level of success, always try to reach back.

In my family, I'm sure no one thought I'd amount to anything. Growing up, I was all over the place. I got in trouble in school. I became a mother while still in high school. At one point,

I even dropped out of school. I was bound to end up in the streets or in prison. I can only imagine what friends and family were saying about me behind my back. I was a disgrace to my family in many ways while in high school. I was dealing with a lot of pain and trauma from my childhood and it affected me in ways beyond words. I was living fast, and by the age of 25, I had gone through more than most women will go through in a lifetime. That's not a stretch of my imagination either. That's the truth, but that's for a later book. I was lost and looking for help but didn't know where to turn.

Then, as a young adult, my life started to change for the better. I got involved in church, got on track and things started looking up. Fast-forward a few years, and I was running my own business. The time came for me to be a leader and I stepped up to the plate. One thing important to me is empowering my family and friends. I don't have a lot of friends because many of those friendships faded along the way during my wild days. But my family has always been there by my side. They haven't always liked me, but they've been there. I got into a position and started to look successful. It was time to call on friends and family for help. I wanted people around me who I could trust, but I also wanted to serve as a blessing to them at the same time. I hired several family members and positioned them in important roles within my company. I leaned on them for support and they leaned on me for support. Sometimes I'd have friends or family come to me and ask for money. I'm not the best at saying no, but I don't like just handing out money either. Money can change people. Money can destroy people. If you ever have to tell someone no, it could destroy your relationship. You have to be mindful of that and pay attention. I've had money destroy my relationships. I would give and give some more. Then when I finally had to say no, those same people viewed me as the worst person in the world. That is never the goal, so I try to empower my friends and family. I want to provide jobs and opportunities. I don't want to feed them. I want to give them an opportunity to get their own food.

Your situation may differ from mine. You may have friends and family who are already qualified to work in your field. It may become your duty to help them get the training needed or to create another opportunity for them. You may have to simply assist them in their field of expertise. We can all do something. If a person wants help, they'll find a way to get it. It's okay to help where you can. Make sure your helping doesn't become a hindrance. That's a mistake we can make sometimes. If we help too much, it can cause people to become complacent. They start expecting handouts instead of getting out and working for what they want need. I want to give the world to my family, but not everyone can handle the world. You can change someone's life, and they can throw it all away. Along the journey, we learn lessons, but if they never got the lessons, they won't know how to handle the blessings. Understand that fact and move with wisdom and caution.

Some of my family members work with me. I like to say "work *with* me" rather than saying, "work *for* me." I don't want them to feel less than. I don't want them to feel like it's only my company. I want them to understand that we are a team and we're building this together. I need their full support and belief in me. If I can empower them and allow them to recognize and realize their worth to the company, they become even better at what they do. So often, people want to be looked up to and praised. We want to be worshipped for the opportunities we've provided, but that's not how it should be. As a leader, you have to be humble. You have to not only aspire to be the best you can be, but also inspire others to be the best they can be.

If a person doesn't want to be empowered, you can't want it for them. You can only help those who want to help themselves. Not everyone wants help. Some people just want attention. Some people want a handout instead of a hand up. You have to recognize the difference. If your support is being squandered, then stop lending assistance to those people. The people who want to help themselves actually need all the help you can give. Be content with helping those people and let the rest come around in their timing. You can't save the world. Not everything you do will be appreciated. Don't lose sleep over those who don't desire growth in their lives.

Go the extra mile. Give help where you can. If you have the ability to help someone you love or care for, do it. I've paid for certification classes for loved ones. I've paid for trainings. I've helped pay for tuition. I've helped buy cars, houses, apartments, and much more. I've done all I can to assist those I love. The things I look for in return are gratitude, effort, and reciprocation of kindness. I don't expect them to do for me on the same level I do for them if I know they are not able. Nothing is worse than doing for someone, and then when you need something from them, they're nowhere to be found. If a person you've helped has it in their power to help you when you need them, and they don't, they just showed you exactly who they are. You will see that in people at times, and those are the people you have to love from a distance. Not everyone can be helped by you and not everyone can work with you.

Don't force anything just because you're related to someone. Bloodline doesn't always make you family. Sometimes your enemies can be your own family. Let everyone show you who they are, and then believe them.

Imagine the feeling to be able to bless those you love and then see them get in a position to no longer need or rely on you. You all will be able to vacation together and everyone pays his or her own way instead of you having to foot the bill. You'll be able to go out to eat or go shopping and not feel drained because you're the only one with money. There's nothing like helping someone you love get into a better position in life.

Look at ways you can assist those you love. If you don't have money to help them, use something else. Give of your time. Give advice. Give love and support. Sometimes just an encouraging word can push someone into his or her rightful place. Don't allow a lack of money stop you from sowing a seed into the life of someone you love. Uplift those around you so you can look others in the eyes instead of only having people looking up to you. Help everyone once you have helped yourself. That is the way we will change the legacy of our families. We have to help put our family members into better positions in their lives. It may not happen for you overnight, but if you keep working, you'll be in a place to help those you love.

Always remember, there's a difference between helping someone and carrying someone. So often people who come from nothing, make it to the top, and then go back to carry their family members. The family can't be carried forever. Everything that goes up will come down, but especially if there's too much weight on you. No matter who you are or what you do, if you try to carry everyone, it will crush you. Careers come to an end.

Circumstances change in every industry. We have to be ready to adjust with the changes. In my industry, funding could fluctuate. That means pay could decrease. If I was carrying my whole family, the bottom would fall out and I could lose it all. That's why it's important to teach others how to fish instead of just giving them fish every day. Your dependents are enough to carry. After that, everyone has to learn how to walk on their own two feet. Don't get caught up and don't lose yourself trying to please everyone. One of the quickest ways to fail is feeling like you have to please everyone around you. Be willing to say no to those who have said no to themselves. Be willing to say yes to those who want to better themselves.

CHAPTER 6

Don't Be Afraid Of Growth

You can't be afraid of growth. Be willing to climb to the next level. There is always more out there. There are always more options, more opportunities and more money to be made. They won't always come to you. You may have to pursue it. Chances are, you're gifted in more than one area of your life. You may have 20 companies in you, but have to build them one at a time. I've studied moguls over the years. I look at their bodies of work and some of them have more than 10 companies under their belts. They may not run them all or even act hands-on in them, but they started and launched them. That inspires me. It helps me realize that it's possible to accomplish many things at once. So many people will tell you to focus on one thing. That's good advice when you're first getting started. After you've found your legs and you're moving along well, you may be ready to start your next venture. You can't fear that growth. It's there to make you better. Don't feel like you have to do everything. Don't get distracted from your true purpose, but know your worth in the marketplace.

Not everyone will understand your ambition because not everyone is you. You will have some family and friends who try to talk you out of your dreams. Listen to reason, but don't listen to pessimism. Don't let a person who is afraid to dream cause your life to be a nightmare. They may not understand your vision because they can't see it from your vantage point. Please understand that just because it doesn't make sense to the people you love, that doesn't mean it's not meant to be. You have to make the final decision and you have to do what you know is best for you. You have to live with the regret, failure or success. So make the decision based on what you feel is best for your future.

I'm still growing. I have a long ways to go. I've had millions of dollars come through my companies so I've seen how money flows. It taught me that anything is possible and there's a marketplace out there full of need and demand. You can build your dream on a small budget and then scale it to something major. No one can stop you, but you.

Why don't we dream bigger? Why are we afraid of growth? I believe we get complacent doing one thing and we fear that anything else we try will fail. We also get trapped in dogma. What others think shouldn't determine your life. Your life needs to be a product of your dreams and desires, not someone else's limitations on your life.

I've gone from business to business and I still have more in me. I've been in the group home space for nearly a decade. I have a system in place that runs itself. I'm at the point where I can focus on other things like this book and some of my other companies. I own a fingerprinting business. I own a consulting firm. I'm opening a real estate investment company and a homebuilding company. I'll continue to grow and expand my brand. I want to bring every idea I have to fruition. I encourage you to live courageously.

There's always a next level and you can't be afraid to go

there. Yes, you can stumble upon something wonderful that makes you a great living. Then after a while, you can grow tired of it and want a change. You may want to be something different or do something different. That is called growth. I once read that the average person has at least four careers in their lifetime. It's not unheard of to switch professions or to evolve into other areas of your gifting. You can't be afraid to grow and expand your brand.

You may stay in the same line of work for 20 or 30 years, and then all of a sudden feel a pull to a new industry and a different type of work. That's okay. I've seen many people shift from a lifetime career and become even more successful in their next stage of life. Some people leave corporate jobs and end up earning more as entrepreneurs. It's not uncommon to improve over time and to use the knowledge you've gained in your industry to help you succeed in another. I've been in business for myself a long time, and I'm just now branching out to write a book. I have many more books in me too. Some authors got started in their early 20's, some even in their teens. It doesn't mean they are any more qualified to write a book than I am. We just took different paths to get here. My book may be more successful than some others who have been writing since their 20's - you never know. Someone may leave their job, enter the group home industry, and blow my company out of the water. You never know how it will play out. Just know you can't be afraid of growth. Your current or past job may have prepared you for your next level. A lot of times people knock the corporate ladder, but I can't knock it. There are valuable lessons to be learned while climbing the corporate ladder that will benefit you when climbing the entrepreneurial ladder, and the same goes for the other way around. Your experiences will strengthen you and teach you the things you need to know for the next level of your life.

If you get complacent, you will eventually be removed. You have to be willing to dig a little deeper and start dreaming a bigger dream. Why are you afraid to launch? What is stopping you from owning two or three companies? They don't all have to earn hundreds of thousands or millions of dollars. You may have one breadwinner and the other company may be a passion project that generates just a few thousand dollars a year. It's not about the money. It's about using your gifts before you lose them.

Someone somewhere is dying to have the gifts you possess. How can you let them sit idle?

I've been behind a desk in my group home for years now. I love the work I do but I know I can do more. I may visit the houses, coach the staff, interact with the consumers, but I don't have too much work to drain my energy or stress me. I have more left in the tank at the end of the day. I can break free and the business can run itself if necessary. I have a solid team and I trust them to execute the vision we've put in place. When I look at my tank, I realize I can burn some oil elsewhere. I have time to busy my hands in other projects. That's why I started OKEY Consulting Group. So many people come to me needing help starting their businesses. They want to know how to get started, what steps to take, how to organize their lives, how to find good people to join them, and so on. I want to help them for free, but free can be draining because not everyone will respect your time. I've put blood, sweat, and tears into building my company and brand, so it's only right that I become a consultant to help others in a professional setting. That's why my consulting company exists. People need me for things outside of the group home. People are calling on me to be their life coach, so I became a certified life coach. People are calling on me to do speaking engagements, so I became a speaker. I have to do what I'm called to do. I have to use my gifts. I can't have people pay my group home for consulting and speaking engagements, so it led to the launching of another company. That's what I mean by growth. You have more in you than you care to admit. You will eventually be pulled in other directions and areas of interest and you have to be willing and ready to go. The company you work for, or the company you're running, may not fit into your next level, so get ready to break out of your shell. Your next level will be calling you if it's not already.

If you're growing weary in what you're doing, that's a sign you can't ignore. You'll begin losing life if you're not living life. You have to be fully engaged and present in your life to get everything out of it. Don't make a move just because someone else made it look pretty. Do it because that's what resonates inside you. I've seen many people quit their job to do something else because they saw someone else become successful at it. Not all success is transferable, especially if it's not your natural gift. Just because someone else is successful in multi-level marketing doesn't mean you'll be successful at it. If it's not your gift or calling, don't do it.

Are you ready to grow? Are you taking heed to your calling? Are you doing all that you can do in your life? Is this it for you, or is there another level waiting on you to step up? It's up to you! Make it happen!

CHAPTER 7

Find Balance

What is life without balance? I'm a mother of four. I love my babies, although they aren't all babies. They need their mother. I'm running errands, chaperoning field trips, doing last minute shopping, cooking, cleaning, movie nights, game nights, and everything in between. To me, that's balance. On a typical day, I will have to work, pick up a kid from school, take one to practice, and attend a game. A day can be so full that my head spins. I need help most days. Thankfully my oldest son is old enough to drive, so he's able to help me out sometimes. That's what it comes down to - balance. I get off at 5pm almost every day. I could sit in the office and find something to do until 9pm if I wanted to, but I have to find balance. I want to be married again one day, so I have to make time for myself too. I have to keep my spirit aligned for my best life, so church is a must. Balance is all of those things.

In our world we're all about work. We believe in work, work, and more work. We glorify the hustle and bustle, and busy is a way of life. We can work ourselves to the bone and still end up broke, lonely and miserable. We are chasing the American Dream, but by the time we get it, it's a nightmare because we don't have balance. I've never admired the hustlers whose faces sink and sag from a lack of sleep. I've never admired the people who can't maintain relationships because they're married to work. I don't want to live my life like that. I know we all make mistakes and no one is perfect, but it's of the essence that you find balance. It does you no good to gain everything and not have peace of mind. I never want my kids to feel like I love anything more than them. What would you gain if you lost your child to drugs or the street life? It doesn't mean it's your entire fault if that happens, but being present will at least give you the peace of mind to know you did all you could. Some days you can't help but work around the clock because there is so much to get done. Those days are important because you show yourself or your family that it takes hard work to be successful in life. They also need to know you have your priorities in order. It's not all about the money. It's not all about the fame and success. It's about family. Family time has to be the most important time to you because when it's all said and done, you'll remember those times more than your work accomplishments.

We've seen the horror stories of kids being left to raise themselves. Maybe you lived that life on one side or the other. If so, you know firsthand what it's like. It's tragic in many cases. I've seen rich kids grow up and go to prison or become addicted to drugs because they never had guidance from their parents who were always too busy. I heard a man say that many parents would rather gift their children $10 instead of 10 minutes. That profound statement has stuck with me ever since. I want to give my kids time over money. Money is nice, but it's replaceable. Time is priceless because it can never be replaced; once it's gone, you can never get it back.

There's a saying that goes, "don't just make a living, make a life." That hit me hard the first time I heard it. I'd become so consumed with business and being successful that I briefly forgot about what matters most. I had to sit down and put myself on notice that my priorities were about to shift. We can give priority to money and toxic relationships sometimes and let the other things that mean the most fall to the wayside. I had to have a gut check and get back on track. Since that time, I've been trying every day to do better at family time.

You may come to a point in your life when you are a big deal and running a very successful operation. You will be obligated to that job and those people. You'll take work home with you. You'll answer emails at the dinner table. You'll ask your lover to hold on a second so you can take a call while on your date. You'll dream about work, and then your alarm clock will wake you up for work. You'll say you're going to relax, but while you're relaxing, you're only thinking about work. Your whole life will become about work, and it will consume you. I read that in some countries, it's against the rules to answer work emails after 5 pm. I try to put that in place for myself. My job requires that I'm available 24 hours a day. I have to be ready to answer the phone at any time. The good thing about it is that the calls don't always last long, and I can put a second-in-command on call if I'm going to be absolutely unavailable. We all have to have boundaries in place so we can create balance. Aim to make a life and not just a living.

I recommend that you take the time to create a concrete schedule. Put your work time on the schedule and then block off time for personal care, and family time. Make sure you treat your personal and family time with the same or more importance than your work time. We rarely interrupt work for personal time, but we're quick to interrupt personal time for work.

I've seen marriages fall apart due to overworking. Men and women completely lose themselves in work and the pursuit of money. Some people deny themselves love to achieve a superficial goal. What were we created for? Were we created to see how much money we can earn? Were we created to see how many trophies we can win? Or were we created to love and replenish the Earth? It's important to know what matters most. Your legacy is in your children, not your job. If you don't have children, your legacy will be in your charity and gift to the world. No one will talk about how hard you worked in a positive way. So make more memories than money. They money will come, but the more you make, the more memories you should make.

On your calendar, create balance. Carve out time to pray, to read, to work out, to spend time with family, and to spend time alone. I learned along the way that God doesn't make mistakes. To make 24 hours in a day, and it not be enough, would have been a big mistake. When I gave my days direction, I realized that 24 hours is more than enough time to do everything I need to do. Like I heard someone say, *"it's not a lack of time, it's a lack of direction."* In order to have increase in your life, you have to have balance. You have to be in balance in every way so you can reap the blessings that have your name on them. If you're too stressed, too worried, or too overworked, you won't be able to give your all and live your best life. So make a plan that creates balance in your life.

No matter what you do, don't get caught up in the hype. Don't believe the lies that you have to work 20 hours days to be successful. You may not even have to work every day. Four hours of focused work is much better than 8 hours of drained, stressed, and frustrated work. You'll do your best work if you have the right balance of work and play.

I am going to be a multi-millionaire mogul one day. It may take me longer, but I'm going to get there on God's timing because I'm seeking balance in my life. I don't want it all overnight. I don't want to work like a slave to live like a Queen. I'll work like a Queen and live like a Queen. Those who can't respect my balance must be removed from my life.

When I speak of balance, I mean mental, emotional, physical, and spiritual. I want my mind, body, and spirit to be right. I work on every area of my life in segments. I can't have an amazing body and leave my mind and spirit behind. I can't have an amazing spirit and mind and leave my body behind. I believe in balance because that gets you the most out of life.

Make your schedule today. Make it fit your life. Don't leave out the important things. Know what matters most and focus on those things first. Everything else will be added to you. You will have peace, love, joy, happiness and success. You can live your best life and achieve your dreams if only you find a healthy balance. Don't work yourself or worry yourself to death. Live your best life!

CHAPTER 8

Protect Your Circle

You have to protect your circle. Who do you have around you? Are they pushing you forward or pulling you down? Think about your relationships. It starts with your intimate partner. If you're in a relationship, evaluate that person. Are they motivating you? Are they pushing you to be better? Are they lifting your spirits and pushing you toward greatness? How do they treat the relationship? Are you settling? It's important that you ask yourself these tough questions. Life is too short to settle for someone who does not treat you with the upmost love and respect. Too many people have settled in a relationship just so they aren't alone. You can't be one of those people. You have greatness in you and you have to live up to your potential. Don't let life get the best of you. Don't let a relationship get the best of you. Pay attention to the signs. If you ignore the signs, you'll end up in a dead-end relationship. So often we ignore the signs and then look up ten years later in a relationship that's killing us. I've been there and I'm begging you not to do the same thing.

I've had to walk away more than once. I gave my all. I fought the good fight, but things didn't turn out right. I don't look down on myself for failed relationships. I realize that I won't tolerate abuse or mistreatment for long. I've been down and out. I was once lost and I tolerated more than anyone should. Then I found my strength. With this strength, I picked myself up and walked away. I walked away and stopped looking back. Today, I'm taking my time in love. I'm not rushing anything. If it's meant to be, it will be. I pay attention to the signs. I'm wiser now. I've lived and I've learned. I've made many mistakes. I can't continue that pattern in this stage of my life. I know my worth and exactly what I bring to the table. Do you know what you bring to the table?

If you're in the dating stage of life, it's even more

important. You have the choice and chance to be picky. It's up to you to write down your standards and decide what type of partner you want in your life. You get to choose. You don't have to settle. Maybe you've already made mistakes in your past. Are you ready for real love? How long are you willing to wait? How much work are you willing to put in yourself to be truly ready? Is it your time? Are there loose ends you need to tie in your life before you get into a relationship? Be honest with yourself. Learn from the past. Heal from the pain. Learn what real love is and start fresh. You have to cut off the people who need to be removed. You have to forgive them and forget them. You can't attract something new if you're holding onto something old. What have you learned from your other relationships or the relationships of your friends and family? Have you truly learned the lessons and implemented the changes or are you still making the same mistakes? This is so important to understand before getting married.

You can have it all, but you can lose it all if you settle down with the wrong person. I've been through it and I've seen many others experience it too. It's one of the most common mistakes people make. We get desperate and lonely and we settle for whoever is in front of us. We ignore the signs and red flags because we think that pain is a part of love. Then we wake up one day and realize that all our relationship has is pain. The love is so little that we can't even feel it. That's never the way to live. Recognize dysfunction early and don't entertain someone who you think will turn on you later. You have too much to lose.

After you evaluate your love life, you have to look at those outside of that. Of your family members, who is good for you? Are there any family members who need to be cut off? Blood doesn't always make you family. There have been times in my life when I've had to step away from family members. Sometimes it may be for just a week or two, but it sends a message. I'm letting them know that I love them, but I love myself more. Refuse to be mistreated or taken for granted. Tell your loved ones that you love you and will help them, but you will not allow anyone to take your kindness for weakness. Tell them not to take you for granted and not to assume that you owe them anything. Let them know you will help if you can, but if you can't, they need to respect that.

Don't let anyone use blood relation as an excuse to use you. You need people around you who would do the same *for* you that they're asking *of* you. One of the biggest mistakes people make is allowing family to use them just because they are related. A lot of people go broke trying to take care of adults who are unwilling to take care of themselves. A common belief is that when one person makes it, the whole family makes it. Empowering your family is a noble concept, but there's a big difference between empowering your family and carrying your family. If you're carrying family members who are able to climb, eventually you'll fall down when you're weak. At that point, will they help you up so you can continue carrying them? Or will they climb off your back, wish you well, and then start climbing on their own? This is a hard truth that many people do not want to face. Most don't want to confront this truth because they feel like they are betraying their family if they stand their ground and demand respect. Requiring respect is the only way to ensure you won't burn yourself out. If you don't respect yourself, no one will do the job for you. Family or not, make sure they appreciate your efforts.

Just as it's important to have good family members in your circle, it's even more important to have good friends in your circle. Most family members will do right by you just because there are unwritten laws between relatives. Friends who are not related to you can be even trickier. These days, the problem with friendships is that they are becoming less genuine. There are a lot of fake friends today and you have to be aware of those individuals. Today, many people want to be associated with those who they feel can get them ahead. They may not care for you at all. They care about what you can do for them. It's the norm in today's society. We live in a microwave society and everyone wants overnight success. Everyone wants instant gratification. That has made genuine friendships rare.

You shouldn't walk around believing that everyone is out to get you, but you have to be mindful and aware. You can believe in the good in people but you can't let the obvious signs go unnoticed. The worst thing that can happen is to have an enemy right next to you. It's dangerous. The people in your circle should want you to win. They should be able to watch you win and not expect to share in the spotlight. If they want the spotlight, they'll learn how to shine in their own right. True friends won't be beggars. They'll find a way to get their own instead of jumping on the bandwagon of our success. If they ask you for something, they'll make sure to pay it back to you. If it's a gift, they won't abuse your giving heart. True friends want to see you win and if you win together, they want it to be because they brought equal to the table. What are they doing for you? What do they bring to the table? They may not have money and gifts, but do they have effort and energy? What are they adding to your life? Are they using you?

With a good friend, you should feel like you don't deserve them at times. It should feel like you're competing to see who can be the better friend. If it's not an equal effort, it's not a real friendship. Be the type of friend you want to attract.

You have to protect your circle. Empower your friends and family, but don't allow anyone in your circle who can derail your life. I've lost enough years from allowing people to get me off track. There's no telling where I could be today had I not wasted so many years with the wrong people in my life. My mistakes birthed this chapter. I protect my circle with intent today. I'm very particular about who I allow into my life. One wrong person can ruin everything you're trying to build. Don't allow people in your life for the wrong reasons. They can be beautiful, rich, connected, and anything else, but if they are toxic, those superficial attributes won't matter.

CHAPTER 9

Break The Mold

We all were put on a path in life. No matter what or where you come from, you have to choose the path at the crossroad of your life. I decided to break the mold. Growing up, I saw poverty all around me. I suffered through a lot of pain that I'll share in a later book. The pain I experienced will shock you and knock you out of your chair. As a young person, I made a lot of mistakes. I was lost, confused and hurting. We went through financial turbulence and a lot of hardships. I honestly don't know how I made it through the struggles of my younger days. I really don't. I can't help but believe in God. There has to be a God for me to be here today. I went through that much. My appearance is not a reflection of what I went through in my life. I made it out on the other side. I believe we all can make it out of adversity. We all can break the mold.

What do you come from? Did your parents set the bar high enough? Are you where you want to be in life? Are you dreaming big enough? Are you just like those who raised you? Or are you better? It's important to ask yourself these questions to determine the direction you will take to solidify your future. You have the power to change your life. It will start with your decisions. I remember when I made the decision to change my life. I had become a product of my pain and was acting from a dark place. I woke up one day and I cried all morning. I'd had enough. I suffered for too long. I had to make a change in my life. I prayed and I prayed some more. I dedicated myself to God and started serving in church. I decided to be a better mother and to give even more love than I was giving. I wanted more. I buckled down in business and I started dreaming bigger and making plans for greatness. I watched my mother work her fingers to the bone all my life and I respected her work ethic, but I wanted more from life. I wanted something grander than just toiling day in and day out. I didn't see any self-made success around me, and I wanted that. Of course, nothing happens without God, but we have to take what he has given us and use it. I decided I would do the work. I applied myself and I kept putting one foot in front of the other. I had to make it. I had to change my life and break the mold. I'd seen all the mistakes of my friends and family. I'd made them all myself too. As a teenage mother, I wasn't supposed to amount to much. I didn't want to be another statistic. I wanted more from life. One good decision led to another good decision. When you string good decisions together, good things happen.

The decision is yours because those who come after you will look up to your example. My mom birthed me as a teen. I birthed my oldest son as a teen. My goal is to not let that be passed down to my children. I want to show them something else in life. In me, they see a strong businesswoman who owns her own. They have everything they need and they see a different type of life than the life I had. I could say I've broken the mold, but the jury is still out on that. I'm not done yet. I'm trying my best to inspire and uplift my children so they can live their legacy. I want to see them flourish and live successful, fulfilling lives. I've done well for myself, but I want to see them do even better. The goal is for my children to build on what I've started. They don't have to work in the same industry, but I want them to know they can be their own bosses and live life on their terms. Nothing is easy. Nothing is for sure, but we can make life into what we want it to be. I'm a firm believer in that, and even if it's not true, I've made it true because I believe in it.

So often we see children become no better than their parents. In many ways, it may be true that we can only do what we know. The beauty of the world is that we can see other examples, even if those examples aren't within reach. We have television, movies and the Internet. We take a look around and see different types of success. That success can inspire us to be more and do more. My mother didn't own her own business, but I saw other women in ownership, and that opened my eyes to the possibilities. Once I saw another woman start her own company, I decided that I could do the same. Now my daughters will know they can own their own companies too. The mold is being broken as we speak. I am rewriting the blueprint with every success and accomplishment.

Decide today that you're going to do more than those who preceded you. If you've already surpassed them, decide to go even further. You can rewrite your family's legacy to be even better. It doesn't matter if you come from alcohol abuse, drug abuse, domestic abuse, crime, or anything else; you can decide today to make a difference. What will it take? Find a mentor, even if you can't talk directly to them. Watch them on YouTube, read their books, or find them in other forums you can get your hands on. Start learning from those who have done what you want to do. Perhaps you were put on an undesirable path in life, but that doesn't mean you have to stay there.

We always hear the stories from millionaires who come from poverty but always dreamed of having more. That inspires me because I had those same dreams and saw them come to pass. We put limits on ourselves. We achieve some success and then we get complacent. We tell ourselves that we've broken the mold and we can kick back and relax. That's not good enough for me. I want more. I want to set the bar so high that my children really have to bust their butts to achieve what I have. I don't want life to be easy for them, nor do I want everything to be handed to them. I appreciate the struggle. They won't have to struggle, but their struggle will come while trying to achieve what I've accomplished in life. I still have a long ways to go. I'm nowhere near where I want to be.

It bothers me to see alcoholics who are the children of alcoholics, or criminals who are the children of criminals. It is disheartening to see people who struggle because that's all they know. I wish I could change it for everyone, but I can't. So I have to focus enough to change it for my household. I don't want any of my children to make the mistakes I made or to experience the pain I've experienced.

There comes a time when you will be tempted to settle. You'll feel like you've done enough. You'll feel like you've done all that you can do. You'll want to settle because going higher is scary. You'll develop a fear of heights because the climb gets more intimidating the higher you go. The air gets thinner near the top. You start to lose friends along the way. Life changes as you go further. You'll be tested and tried but you have to decide every day what you're doing to do. I'm making a decision today to turn it up a notch. It's the first day of the New Year and I'm walking in my dreams. I'm getting closer to doing bigger things. This book is a part of the next level for me. My new company is a part of the next level for me. There is always temptation to sell my businesses and go back to working for someone else so I don't have to stress or worry about all the things that come with owning a business, but in that moment of weakness, I make the conscious decision to get stronger. Quitting is unacceptable. I think about the people who are struggling with drugs, criminal behavior and other bad habits. I see all the examples of people who became products of their environment and ended up in prison or the grave. I run those images through my mind daily. I think about the women who settled for abusive lovers and now are stuck with men who don't love them or block them from being great. I think about all the ways I can remain stuck and I want more. I could almost cry when I think about all that I had to overcome to write this book. I think about all the naysayers and haters. I think about my legacy that I'll leave and it brings tears to my eyes. To say I'm blessed is an understatement.

I want you to understand that you're not reading this by

chance. This is divine. This is your chance to step up and go further. You can do more in your life but you have to really decide that you're going to break the mold. Write your plan today. Put it up on the wall and look at it every day. Tell your friends to strive for more. Tell your family to strive for more. Become a legacy builder through the encouragement of those you love. Impact the world with your life and God-given gifts. What are you going to do? Are you going to settle? Is good, good enough for you? Do you want more? Do you want better for your life? If your mother or father has gone on to glory, make sure they can look down and smile at the work you're doing. If they are still living, make sure they see you fulfill your potential while they're still with you. Believe and keep pressing. You can absolutely shift your life for the better and realize your dreams. Don't make any more excuses. Don't blame anyone else any longer. Look in the mirror and decide that it's up to you and then do what it takes to make it happen. The struggle will always be there. You won't be able to escape the trials and tribulation. You'll be tempted and tested at every turn to give up, but you can't. There is someone watching you. They are studying your every move because you're their hope. If that's your child watching, then your journey is even more important. It's up to you to make it happen and you won't be able to hold anyone else accountable for your shortcomings. Once you gain the knowledge of your own power, you have to accept it and take on the call to go further in your life. Don't let your negative self-talk stop you from living life to the fullest. Don't allow anything to hold you back. Cut people off today if you need to. Decide today that your vices will no longer control your life. Make a decision that you'll be more than just a social security number. Don't waste another minute. Take action today!!

NOTE FROM THE AUTHOR

I thank you so much for reading this book. This is only the beginning. I didn't want to get too heavy in this book. I have so much more to say and it gets so deep that I didn't want to jump right into it in my first book. I hope you heard my heart. I hope this has inspired you even if but a little to live your dreams. If I can do it, I feel like anyone can.

Please share this book with someone who needs it. You never know what it would mean to someone who is in the midst of his or her life's storm. It could be one sentence that shifts and changes someone's mindset. This has meant a lot to me writing this intro book. I hope to continue to work with you over the years. If you have any questions or comments, please don't hesitate to write me.

God bless you,

Donishia